THE DK POCKET GUIDE TO
GOLF

E

Sharon
To My Favorite
Scratch Golfer!
Dave

THE **DK** POCKET GUIDE TO

· GOLF ·
ETIQUETTE

MALCOLM CAMPBELL

DK PUBLISHING, INC.

A DK PUBLISHING BOOK

•

Produced for DK Publishing by
COOLING BROWN

Managing Editor Francis Ritter
Managing Art Editor Derek Coombes

First American Edition, 1997
2 4 6 8 10 9 7 5 3 1

Published in the United States by
DK Publishing, Inc.
95 Madison Avenue
New York, New York 10016
Visit us on the World Wide Web at
http://www.dk.com

Copyright © 1997
Dorling Kindersley Limited
Text copyright © 1997
Malcolm Campbell

A catalog record is available from the
Library of Congress

ISBN 0-7894-1467-8

Color reproduction by
Colourscan, Singapore
Printed in Hong Kong
by Wing King Tong Co. Ltd.

CONTENTS

•

FOREWORD

INTRODUCTION 8

FOREWORD

THERE CAN BE few things more irritating, and at times even infuriating, for a golfer than to find his game ruined by thoughtless and ignorant behavior by other players on the course. This book by Malcolm Campbell will be invaluable to all golfers, both new participants and experienced players alike, and will serve as a convenient reminder to all of the importance of the unwritten rules of the game.

At a time when there is an increasing interest in golf, stimulated by high-profile professionals appearing on television, there is an obvious danger of inappropriate behavior by spectators also. This book, by an author who is vastly experienced both as a player and as a communicator, can only make a wider audience more aware of correct conduct on the golf course, allowing everyone to enjoy the game to the fullest.

DR. A. M. MATHEWSON
CAPTAIN OF THE ROYAL & ANCIENT
GOLF CLUB OF ST. ANDREWS

ENJOYING GOLF TO THE FULLEST
*A peaceful scene surrounds Andrew Sherbourne at
Gleneagles during the Scottish Open in 1989, but it is only
awareness of correct behavior by golfers and spectators
alike that can assure this continuing peace.*

INTRODUCTION

SIMPLY BECAUSE AN INDIVIDUAL owns some golf clubs and a few golf balls, and takes them on to a golf course to put one to the other in the accepted fashion, it does not follow logically that that person is by definition a golfer. There is far more subtlety to the ancient game of golf than that.

Golf is as much, or perhaps even more, about *how* it is played as it is about *how well* it is played. In the five hundred years or so that golf as we know it has been around, the game has developed, not just as a simple pastime of club and ball, but into what is for many a way of life.

ETIQUETTE AND RULES
Etiquette is all about courtesy and common sense tied in with a sound grasp of the basic rules.

CODES OF COMMON CONDUCT

That way of life is governed by a strict code of rules known as the Rules of Golf; but in addition another code applies – it is a code of ethics, principles, and behavior called the "etiquette" of the game. *The Concise Oxford Dictionary* describes "etiquette" as "the conventional rules of personal behavior in polite society" and in addition describes "polite" as "courteous" and "of refined manners."

This may be the lexicon of another era but is the real clue to the development of golf as the game of high moral code, personal integrity, good behavior, and above all, respect for the fellow competitor. The great traditions in golf have emerged from centuries of devotion to these basic principles of honest play and good manners.

These principles have been firmly ingrained because of a strong golf establishment that has at times dealt harshly with those who cannot, or will not, conform. Some golf officials are accused of being reactionary,

FAIR PLAY
For professional or amateur players, fair play and good sportsmanship are integral parts of golf etiquette.

but it is only because of golf's commitment to its unwritten codes – as well as to its written rules – that it has been able to resist the forces that have had such an adverse effect on so many other sports.

PRESSURES ON THE GAME

Golf remains the "clean" game, although its reputation is not totally unsullied: court cases that followed disputes between players on fairways here and overseas, and even a fatal shooting on the first tee of a golf club in Buffalo, are all testament to that. These are worrying trends for golf administrators all over the world trying to cope with masses of newcomers to the world's fastest-growing sport.

There was a time when most new players learned the unwritten rules of

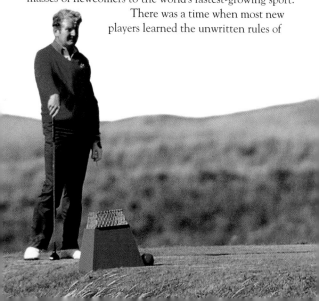

conduct and the wider principles of the game from the
experience of others. Today this is less often the case.
The great golf boom of the 1980s created such an influx
of new players desperate to be part of a game that had
suddenly become fashionable that the established clubs
and public courses could not cope with the demand.

In the case of private clubs, the absence of
membership openings has led to lengthy waiting lists for
admission. In addition, the increased demand has
invariably led to higher membership costs. Today, in

COURTESY AND SAFETY
*Stand back and well beyond the
arc of your partner's swing when
he or she is teeing off. Players
can underestimate the reach of
a club's arc.*

major metropolitan areas of the United States, it is not unusual for initiation fees to cost tens of thousands of dollars. At the same time, the tremendous growth of golf's popularity – fueled in no small part by the large numbers of women taking up the game – has placed additional pressures on public and semiprivate courses. In many parts of the country starting times, even during the week, are at a premium.

THE EFFECTS OF GOLF'S GROWTH

The result of golf's growing popularity is that large numbers of people are taking up the game without a sufficient background in the game's rituals, traditions, and codes of behavior. In the past, these were ingrained in people who were attracted to the game as either junior golfers or caddies and thus were able to learn from the example set by adults.

As a result, the explosion in the number of new golfers, while welcome, has increasingly challenged the traditional nature of the game. Increasingly, slow play has become a problem, and the ensuing frustration has

occasionally led to a decline in respect for both other players and for the condition of the courses themselves. In addition, ignorance of these traditions can make an already difficult game even more intimidating.

It is for these reasons that this book exists. I hope to lay out for the first time the main principles that have been valued in golf for

FINDING ADDED VALUE
Clever solutions to the physical pressures on the sport do not address the problem of learning the "values" of the game.

so many decades, and in doing so explain why golf will remain the most ethical of all sports only as long as those who play it not only respect its traditions but also do their utmost to uphold them.

This guide is therefore a reaffirmation and re-dedication to these principles for the already established player, and hopefully a book that will help the newcomer to the game to understand the responsibilities that come with being part of the world of golf. The chapters that follow provide an easy reference to the mysteries of golf etiquette and will help the newcomer to integrate quickly into the wider aspects of the game.

Unlike the actual Rules of Golf, the codes, etiquette, and principles of golf are not codified. They rely upon a common consent and attitude of mind. Without a genuine commitment to both, the mere striker of a golf ball cannot hope to join the ranks of the golfer.

If this volume contributes even a little to a better understanding of the true and traditional nature and spirit of the game, I will be content.

MALCOLM L. CAMPBELL
LOWER LARGO, SCOTLAND

SPECTATOR ETIQUETTE
Being a golf tournament spectator brings with it its own standards of acceptable and unacceptable behavior.

CHAPTER ONE

WHAT *is* GOLF ETIQUETTE?

THE RULES OF GOLF as approved by the
Royal & Ancient Golf Club of St. Andrews
and the United States Golf Association make very
little reference to the etiquette of golf. The Rules
of Golf contain only a few lines on courtesy,
priority on the course, and care
of the golf course itself.

But within these categories there is
much in the way of unwritten convention that
those who wish to be taken seriously as golfers
must understand and absorb. This chapter
explains the reasons behind the written and
unwritten rules of golf; that is, the etiquette.

B

GUARDIAN OF GOOD CONDUCT
*St. Andrews in Scotland is the spiritual home of golf,
and one of the key administrative centers for deciding
upon golf disputes and interpretations of the rules.*

CODES *of* CONDUCT

I T WAS THE SCOTS who not only drew up the first basic set of rules – thirteen in all – but who also evolved the codes of conduct and standards of behavior among its participants that have earned golf its reputation as the most ethical and disciplined game of them all.

THE WRITTEN RULES

The first written rules of golf were formulated by the Gentlemen Golfers of Leith, now the Honourable Company of Edinburgh Golfers, in 1744. However, for some time afterward new clubs continued to draw up their own

rules for play until, in 1897, the Royal &
Ancient Golf Club of St. Andrews (R&A),
was invited by the leading clubs of the day to
compile a uniform code of rules. Today the
R&A, in conjunction with the United States
Golf Association (USGA), administer the
Rules of Golf and make decisions on these
rules for golfers all over the world.

Decisions on the Rules of Golf is published
jointly by the two organizations and revised
annually. It first appeared in 1984, and
marked a breakthrough in R&A–USGA
cooperation. A Joint Decisions Committee
meets every four years to review the written
Rules of Golf.

**SCOTTISH SELF-
DISCIPLINE**
*By the early
1890s the rules
and standards of
play in Scotland
were well
developed, if
not codified. The
poorer condition
of the greens in
those days made
leaning on the
clubs less critical
than it is today.*

A ROYAL AND ANCIENT GAME
What started as a sport for the wealthy has now become a sport for all. Golf etiquette balances this sense of tradition with the modern need for fast play.

UNWRITTEN RULES OF GOLF

While the rules of play are well documented, there is no written account of the long established codes of etiquette and behavior that are so much part of the game of golf. These codes have evolved over two centuries since the official Rules of Golf were established and greater organization came into the game.

In the early days of organized golf the cost of equipment, particularly the feathery ball, dictated that for the most part it was the

wealthy gentlemen of the time who formed the great majority of those playing.

The social order of the time, which provided an established gentleman with a manservant, was reflected in golf in the teaming of player and caddie. The strict codes of honor and social behavior of that era, influenced considerably by the educational and, often, military standards of those who played, spilled over into the game itself.

In golf these unwritten but understood codes have survived social and industrial revolution and remain intact today as the etiquette of the game.

ETIQUETTE FOR EVERYONE
The early influence of women golfers helped reinforce the notions of good behavior on and off the course.

Today, the etiquette of golf revolves around the principles of playing responsibilities, social aspects, and understanding the rules. It is the commitment to grasping and upholding the principles governing these key areas (*see box opposite*) that separates the golfer from the mere hitter of golf balls.

COLLECTIVE CODES
Established golf clubs have friendly matches and club events that help engender an esprit de corps.

LEARNING FROM FRIENDS

Newcomers to the game who are fortunate enough to be able to join an established golf club or course have the advantage of learning these principles from the members with whom they come into contact in competitions, friendly matches, and in the clubhouse.

Those who are not fortunate enough to be able to join a club or have access to a good public course have much less opportunity to understand what the game expects from them. However, the newcomer must first forget the sometimes-held view that the game is run by squads of pompous, aging gentlemen in regimental ties just looking for an excuse to parade their own importance.

GOLF ETIQUETTE

Etiquette in golf governs four main aspects of the game:

The golfer's relationship with his partners or fellow competitors

•

The golfer's responsibilities to the course on which he plays

•

The social aspects of the game before and after play

•

Knowledge and respect for the written rules of the game

THE GAME OF RESPECT
In truth, there may be the odd officious example, but for the most part the game of golf is populated by ordinary men and women who have respect for one another, respect for the environment in which they play, and respect for the traditions of honorable endeavor that attracted them to golf in the first place. As it is, golf is much more about self-control and self-regulation than it is about having others administer it for you.

There is no place in the game for those who wish to bring to it a boorish mentality. But those who believe in honesty and integrity in sport and decent standards of behavior will find many fellow travelers in golf.

CHAPTER TWO

AT *the* GOLF COURSE

JUST AS THERE ARE conventions to be observed when we visit other people's homes, so there are accepted rules of behavior when we visit the golf club. This applies as much to arriving at our own golf course as it does to a visit to any other. There is a pattern of accepted behavior on and off the course, and in the clubhouse, which is sensible and considerate of others and has evolved over the years. It might seem more formal at one place than another, or differ in matter of detail, but essentially the same principles apply wherever the game is played. The following chapter is a useful guide for the considerate golfer.

LEARN FROM THE MASTERS
Watching the Masters from Augusta, Georgia, can teach you as much about etiquette and temperament among the top players as it can about techniques.

ARRIVAL *at the* COURSE

T HE INFLUENCE OF established conventions exerts itself from the minute we arrive at the golf course. When we park the car, we don't drive into the best spot beside the clubhouse and ignore the sign that reminds us that the spot has been reserved for others. And yet some people do.

DON'T BE THOUGHTLESS

Car parking spaces have been allocated to officials as a courtesy, and in recognition of the contribution they make to the running of the course on behalf of those who play there.

At the Barossa Golf Club in the South Australian bush, where the golf facilities are by most standards quite basic, one club official has left culprits of basic discourtesy in no doubt as to where they stand. The sign on the chain-link fence depicts a hooded axeman alongside the legend "Park Here at Your Own Risk." It is signed rather ominously in blood-red letters "Handicapper"! As a deterrent it seems to work admirably, but the simple fact is that it should not have been necessary to erect it at all. Wherever you play, don't be inconsiderate; park where you are meant to.

MEMBERS OF ROYAL & ANCIENT GOLF CLUB ONLY

READ THE SIGNS
Heed the club signs and directions – wherever you play.

ORDER FOOD IN ADVANCE

*An important point before leaving the clubhouse for the course:
if you want to have a meal when you come in after a game, let the
staff know in advance. It's a small point but a simple courtesy,
and it guarantees that you will be expected when you come in
from your round.*

WHERE TO CHANGE YOUR SHOES

Where we change into our golf shoes is
probably more of a geographic consideration
than one of propriety in world golf. In Europe,
most golf clubs prefer their members and
visitors to change into golf clothes and put on
their golf shoes in the locker room rather than
in the parking lot – although it is by no means
true of them all.

GOLF SHOES
*There are places
for spikes and
places where they
shouldn't go. Be
considerate when
changing your
shoes.*

In the United States, most players
arrive at the golf club dressed for play
anyway. However, shoes are often
changed in the parking lot, or when
the golf bag is taken to the first tee.

Nevertheless, it is incumbent upon
all players to establish what
convention demands at a particular
course and have the courtesy to respect
it. Even if your own course has no
objection to you changing your shoes
in the parking lot, do not take upon
yourself the right to adopt that
procedure at every other course you
play. Again, when you arrive at a new
course, check for signs regarding the
use of golf shoes.

DRESS SENSE

There are perhaps more arguments over dress code at golf courses – especially private clubs – than over anything else. The wearing of blue denim jeans, however expensive the designer label, T-shirts, and sneakers is the one thing that sends more people into incandescent rage than any other.

For players who feel none of these dress variations have any place on a golf course, even the way a newcomer wears his hat (e.g., a cap back to front) can be a major source of irritation.

In the clubhouse, the demand of many clubs that a jacket, collar, and tie must be worn in the lounge or dining room of the golf club can get golfers literally hot under the collar. The length above the knee of ladies' shorts, and the strange insistence of some clubs that men may wear shorts only in tandem with knee-length socks, are

FANCY DRESS
While it is common sense that T-shirts and jeans should not be worn, you do not have to go to the extremes of flamboyant dress sense shown by Payne Stewart.

SIGN LANGUAGE
Strict dress codes apply at some golf clubs, as this sign at Las Brisas, Spain, graphically points out.

two other common bones of dress-code contention regularly debated.

The point to be made here is not whether these rules, formally laid down by the committees or simply as accepted convention, are right or wrong. Whether we agree with them or not, they are the rules of engagement until such times as they are changed, and as such common courtesy demands that they be respected.

Club members who disagree with rules laid down by their committee on dress code, or anything else to do with the way the club is run, have the power to change them through the club's constitution. Nonmembers have the right to choose a club where the rules on dress may be more to their liking.

No one has the right simply to ignore the rules and go their own sweet way. Therein lies the road to anarchy.

KNEE LENGTH
Some clubs are fussy about the length of ladies' shorts, some are not; however, club codes must be adhered to.

USE YOUR YARDAGE BOOK

Most golf courses now have a guidebook that gives information on the yardages on every hole, measured from fixed points such as bunkers, trees, or other landmarks to the green. Sometimes known as "Strokesavers" (although this is, strictly speaking, the name of only one of several manufacturers), these booklets are particularly useful for players visiting courses they have not played or visited before.

In addition to the yardage measurements, these booklets also provide a diagram of the individual holes, depicting the hazards and other relevant information such as out-of-bounds fences.

Club guidebooks are also a useful record of the clubs you visit in the course of your golfing career.

CHECK BEFORE YOU PLAY
Useful information about teeing areas and distances to trees and sprinkler heads may be shown in yardage books. This is the 13th hole at Augusta National.

0
10yds (9m)
30yds (26m)
40yds (37m)

225yds
(206m)

Rae's Creek

38yds (35m)

BECOME SECURITY CONSCIOUS

It's a sad reflection of the times we live in that we have to be conscious of the security of our possessions at all times. This is just as true of the golf club as anywhere else, particularly at European courses, where there is less security than may be expected at the majority of American golf clubs.

- *Don't leave golf clubs outside the locker room while you go into the clubhouse for a drink or a meal after your game.*

- *It takes only a couple of minutes to put the golf bag back in the trunk. Short of a mobile bank vault, that is the safest place for it.*

- *Use a small felt or leather bag to store items such as your watch, car keys, and loose change in the golf bag. It keeps them safe and saves having to fish around in the bottom of pockets in the golf bag after the round.*

BRUSH OFF AFTER PLAY

Is the trunk of your car constantly covered in loose grass and mud from your golf shoes or the wheels of your cart? It is? Then get yourself an old cardboard box and a household handbrush and keep them in the car. A few seconds spent brushing off dirt and grass from shoes and wheels will save lots of car-cleaning time.

BE READY *to* TEE OFF

I N THE HUMDRUM of modern life golf, for most players, has to be fitted into a busy schedule. But that should not mean turning up to play with only seconds to spare before your tee time, totally unprepared for the game you have taken the trouble to book.

CHECK EQUIPMENT BEFORE PLAY

How many times have you had to scramble around looking for a tee on the first hole, or had to search for your glove while the other three members of your foursome have already driven and are waiting patiently for you to catch up? A few seconds' thought to check the items you need to play saves time and your own embarrassment. It's also better for your blood pressure.

Tardiness at the first tee is not only bad for your game, it's bad manners. Friends, colleagues, or competitors with whom you are playing will almost certainly have just as tight schedules as you do, and it is quite unsettling for the other members of the group if the last player runs onto the tee with his golf shoes still untied, pulling on his sweater.

It is common courtesy to make sure you are punctual for your game, and it also gives you the best chance to play well.

BE AWARE AND OBSERVANT
Remember the order you are playing in, and be courteous enough to watch the other players' shots closely to confirm the direction in which they went.

WARM-UP EXERCISES

Make time to get to the course a little earlier to warm up golf muscles that may not have been used for a week, or maybe even hit a few practice shots. Would a sprinter rush up the track, jump out of his car and into the starting blocks with his muscles cold and the laces of his running spikes untied? Of course not, and neither should the weekend golfer rush onto the tee similarly unprepared.

TWO-CLUB SWING

WRISTS
Keep a constant light grip and try not to hinge the wrists

CLUBS
Swing two clubs together

SHOULDERS
Feel the weight of two clubs through your arms to shoulder

WAIST
Feel the hips respond to the full turn of the shoulders and upper body

KNEES
Allow the knee to come in naturally

REMEMBER

Don't turn up on the first tee and then start all your upper-body strengthening exercises or practice swings. This is both dangerous and a distraction.

TRUNK ROTATION

PLATFORM
Place a golf club behind your neck

GRIP
Take a firm but not too tight hold

1 Standing with your feet shoulder-width apart, rest a club on the back of your neck and take a light grip of both ends.

2 Keep eyes firmly fixed in front of you and turn your trunk to the left as if in your backswing. Your hips remain in a constant position.

3 Return to the start position and make a turn in the opposite direction, as if you were following through. Hold. Repeat six times.

PRACTICE SWING WITH SAFETY

The Rules of Golf warn of the danger of swinging without consideration for fellow players standing nearby. This is also common sense. Although it should not need stressing that a golf club swung in anger is a highly dangerous implement, there are many recorded instances of serious injury to players struck by a carelessly swung club. It may seem to be stating the obvious, but ensure that you are standing well clear when a fellow player is teeing off. Far too many

CHECK BEHIND YOU
Even though your playing partner should be looking out himself as you address the ball, double-check that he is not in danger before a practice swing.

golfers have been injured on the tee by golf
balls that have come off the clubface in
the wrong direction.

▷ PICK UP, DON'T HIT UP
*Don't swing at loose stones or other
debris, such as pine cones or pieces
of broken twigs.*

▽ BE WARY OF THE BACKSWING
*Don't stand too close to a fellow player when
he or she is taking a practice swing. Be alert.*

AWAITING YOUR TURN

The correct place to stand when a fellow player is teeing off, or hitting a fairway shot, is always to the side and behind the right angle of the intended flight line of the ball (*see bottom illustration*).

◁ **DANGER...**
Do not stand directly behind the ball when a player is addressing the ball or playing a stroke.

◁ **...AND DISTRACTION**
Do not stand in a position that will distract the player.

STAY ALERT

When a golf ball leaves the clubface on a full shot it becomes a very dangerous missile. In many cases it is a misguided missile. Sadly there are many recorded fatalities from players struck by golf balls. A golfer simply cannot be too careful. Always be ready to call "fore" if you think your ball, or that of a fellow player, is in any danger of hitting another player or person on the course.

WATCH OUT FOR YOUR PARTNER
Always watch the flight of the ball of a fellow player. You may need to help them find it if it goes off line.

CHAPTER THREE

PACE *of* PLAY

IN THE FIRST BOOK on golf published in the United States in 1895, *Golf in America: A Practical Manual*, the author, James P. Lee, explained the background to a "new game that has been added to the list of outdoor sports." Lee also made the observation: "There is no racing or any effort to accomplish a hole in less time than your opponents." It is a valid point, but although golf is not a sprint, neither is it a crawl. This chapter is therefore all about saving time and speeding up play. Maintaining the speed of the course is vital to everyone's enjoyment. It is also important to optimize the number of people that can get around a golf course in a given period of time, since the pressures on golf course space are increasing all the time.

Ironically, the average time taken to play a round of golf seems to increase year by year. There are many factors contributing to this, the single biggest problem in the game. In this chapter we look at how the responsible and considerate golfer can help to speed up play for the better enjoyment of all.

RITUAL AGAINST REASON
To speed up play, ask yourself, "Do I really need to take off my golf glove in order to execute an effective putt?" You don't always have to mimic the professionals.

ON *the* TEE

RULE 6-7 OF THE Rules of Golf demands that "the player shall play without undue delay and in accordance with any pace of play guidelines laid down by the (Club) Committee." There are in fact penalties for a breach of this rule, as witnessed occasionally in professional golf tournaments, but sadly they are seldom if ever imposed at the amateur level, despite a very clear need for them to be rigorously enforced.

SMART MOVES

- After finishing a hole, move quickly to the next tee.
- Do not stand on the green and mark the scores for the hole. Do it while waiting your turn to play on the next tee.
- On the tee, be ready to play as soon as the group in front is out of range.

- Do not stand over a ball forever. A player who appears paralyzed when addressing the ball causes frustration to his fellow player and reduces his chance of making a good stroke. If you are going to miss it, sage advice is to miss it quickly.

◁ TO WAIT OR NOT TO WAIT?
Even though in the rules you are allowed to play when the group in front has completed their second shot, use your common sense to judge whether it is safe.

SPEED WITH SAFETY

The golfer must take responsibility for the speed of play and for trying to reverse a trend toward slowness against which there is virtually unanimous agreement. Having said that, it is equally common sense, as well as common courtesy, to wait until the players ahead have played and moved out of range.

Unfortunately, there remains a belief among those less considerate players that, when they stand on the tee, this point of safety is reached when the players in front have all played their second shots. This is not necessarily the case.

Different skill levels in the game require that some players will need two shots to get safely out of range of the players behind. Be patient, considerate, and above all, be safe, by recognizing that fact and giving that little extra time when it is required. Everyone wants to keep play moving, but safety must never be compromised.

ON *the* FAIRWAY

CONSIDERABLE SAVINGS CAN be made in time if everyone in the group plans the shot they have to play as they approach their ball. Don't stand around watching everyone else play before deciding what the problems are that you face yourself. Gauge your shot while your opponents are playing theirs. It saves time and doesn't prevent you from seeing the outcome of their shots before you play.

ON THE MOVE
Professionals have the time, and caddies, to help them calculate the yardage. You don't, so make sure you work it out as you approach the ball.

CHECK THE YARDAGE

If you tend to benefit from the use of yardage information, save additional time by using the available data on the distance to the hole.

Check your yardage book as you walk up to the ball. It wastes time to wait until you get

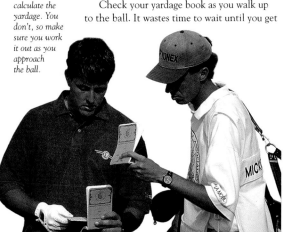

there before fishing out the reference book and starting the search.

If there is one, look for the 150-yard marker as you walk down the fairway. Alternatively, check for the distances marked on sprinkler heads in the fairway if that is available. Don't wait until you get to your ball before starting to look for them.

REDUCE PRACTICE SWINGS

Another major contributor in slow play is the golfer who insists on playing four rounds of golf every time he goes out on the course. His round is made up of every stroke he plays plus the three practice swings he takes before every shot!

A brief, simple swish of the club to release tension and give a mental picture of the swing should be all that is required.

The golf player who habitually and meticulously addresses an imaginary ball, takes several looks down the fairway as he hovers interminably over the ball before making a practice swing – and then repeats the process twice more before preparing to play his shot – is golf's public enemy number one.

Such actions go against good etiquette and, sadly, are often a product of a teaching system that concentrates almost exclusively on the techniques of the game. Just as important is to know what is expected of the golfer on the course – especially when it comes to the finer points of getting around during the available hours of daylight!

Let Faster Players Through

There are three factors that have a major impact on the speed of play on a golf course:

- *How players react to losing their place on the course by dropping behind the group in front.*

- *How players react to a faster group playing behind.*

- *How players deal with a possible lost ball situation.*

PLAYING THROUGH
Letting players through keeps the pace of play up, and it removes the distraction of a group constantly pressing from behind. The few minutes involved in allowing a faster group to pass through are more than compensated for by the removal of a major distraction.

LOOKING FOR LOST BALLS

Perhaps the worst time-wasting offense is committed by the players who selfishly insist on looking for lost golf balls while holding up, not only the players immediately behind them, but, by extension, the whole course.

If a player feels that there is any danger of his ball not being found, he should immediately announce his intention and then play a provisional ball under the Rules.

If the original ball is not found, a provisional ball saves a frustrating and embarrassing walk back to where the original ball was played from in order to put another in play.

The Rules of Golf allow a player five minutes to look for a lost ball, *but the time to call through the group behind is not after five minutes have been spent looking for the ball.* If the ball is not found immediately, the group should be called through at that point and the five minutes used for the search while the group plays through.

There is nothing in the Rules of Golf that covers any of these factors, but the accepted conventions of the game, established over many generations, are quite clear.

Any group losing its place on the course, that is, dropping a full hole behind the match in front, for whatever reason, should quickly take steps to close the gap. If they fail to do so, they should stand aside and allow the match behind through.

If the course ahead is clear, any group holding up the players behind should stand aside and allow the following match to play through. It is simple courtesy to call through a single, pair, or group of players as soon as it is apparent their match has fallen behind.

On *the* Green

THE PUTTING GREEN is the scene of some of the worst examples of wasted time on the golf course. The televising of professional golf has encouraged amateur players to mark, lift, and clean their golf balls before almost every putt.

WHEN TO MARK

It should only be necessary for the amateur player to mark and lift his ball:

- *If it is interfering with the line of a fellow player's putt.*

- *If there is dirt adhering to it which might deflect the ball from its intended line.*

- *If it lies in such a position that to take his putting stance a player would stand on the line of a fellow player's putt.*

HOW TO MARK THE BALL

If it is necessary for the ball to be marked and lifted, its position must be clearly marked by placing a coin or marker immediately behind the ball before lifting it from the putting surface.

Place the marker

Replace the ball

MOVING THE MARKER

If a ball marker interferes with the play, stance, or stroke of another player, it must be moved. By following this simple method of moving a marker (*below*), you ensure that you will always be lifting and replacing it on the correct spot.

1 *Tell your partner what you propose to do. Then place the toe of your putter immediately behind the marker, lining up the head of the club with a clearly defined object, such as a distinctive tree, post, or a tee box in the distance.*

2 *Move the marker from the toe of the club to the heel of the club. The marker may be moved several clubhead lengths in this manner. In extreme cases, the shaft of the putter may be used as a distance gauge to move the marker.*

COPYING THE PROFESSIONALS

Everyone may want to be Tiger Woods, Nick Faldo, or Greg Norman, but copying the professionals can cost time that the game cannot afford if golf courses are to accommodate the numbers of golfers who want to play.

The trend set by Arnold Palmer (*see box opposite*) in his heyday has today reached epidemic proportions, to the point where players ritually remove their glove and replace it after almost every shot.

With the aid of caddies, professionals can remove and replace gloves to their heart's content as they walk down the fairway, unencumbered by equipment that the rest of us have to transport for ourselves.

GLOVES-OFF TIME
If you are one of those players who simply must remove the glove before putting, do so while walking onto the green and lining up the putt. Don't wait until it is your turn to putt before starting the disrobing process.

PALMER-STYLE PUTTING

When Arnold Palmer was at the height of his powers in the 1960s, he would remove his glove before putting, fold it neatly, and slip it into the back pocket of his slacks with the fingers of the glove hanging symmetrically downward. So began a fashion among amateur golfers that persists to this day, encouraged again by televised professional golf, which shows, with only a few notable exceptions, players constantly removing gloves.

CONVENTION OR NECESSITY?
Be wary of the trend set by Arnold Palmer of painstakingly removing the glove for every putt.

Inevitably, of course, the fashion has spread into the amateur game, resulting in huge amounts of time lost in the removal and replacement of gloves.

GOLF GLOVE ETIQUETTE

Removing your golf glove while putting can at best have only an infinitesimal effect on the outcome of the putt. For the professional it may make a difference; for the amateur golfer playing simply for enjoyment it is difficult to see how the tiny potential benefit can justify the time involved in this cumbersome process.

DON'T PROWL THE GREEN

Time can be saved by paying attention to the following simple advice: Assess the line of the putt while walking to the ball. Don't prowl the green.

Viewing a putt from every angle and stalking it like a big-game hunter may say lots for your commitment, but the likelihood is that it will do very little to improve your chances of holing the putt. First impressions are usually best. Spend too much time and you simply add to the confusion.

▽ PICTURE
AND PUTT
Make sure you assess the line of your putt as you approach the green. Don't wait until you get there.

IF IN DOUBT, PUTT OUT

Don't waste time marking tap-in putts. Unless you are going to stand directly on another player's line, tap the short ones in, taking sufficient care of course, and move on.

Continuous putting, in which each player putts until he has holed out, is one of the best ways to save time on the greens.

The one possible exception to this point of etiquette might be in some matchplay situations where tactical putting may become a factor.

◁ **BIG GAME**
*Make your decision
based on first
impressions. Don't
waste time viewing
the putt from
every angle.*

OFF *the* GREEN

WHERE ONCE UPON a time golfers had caddies to carry their golf bags, changes in society and equiment have changed that traditional part of the game. As in so many other walks of life, technology has now taken over the elementary tasks of labor.

GOLF CART PARKING

The pull cart, still seen on some courses, and the motorized golf cart (synonymous with golf for many people) have had an impact on the speed at which the game is now played.

If players do not think and act sensibly in their use of these devices, whether two-wheeled or four, the cost in terms of unnecessary time spent on the course can be high. Just a little thought and consideration for the players behind saves time and frustration.

GOLF CART TIPS

The following simple rules help to keep delays to a minimum:

- *Always leave pull carts at the closest point on the direct route from the green to the next tee.*
- *Leaving the cart at the front of the green, as so many unthinking players do, simply means delay while the player walks back to retrieve it. During this wasted period at least one of the next group could have played his approach to the green and kept play moving a little more quickly.*
- *Motorized golf carts should also be left at the exit to the green and not in front of it.*

MARK THE CARD OFF THE GREEN

The place to mark down your playing partner's score is not on the green after everyone has holed out. Don't linger on the green to work out the score – you have finished putting, so get off the green!

Newcomers to the game, anxious to make sure they accurately count the strokes taken, are the most common culprits, but they must understand that a player standing on a green, gesturing to the various points visited on the route to the green along fairway or rough, counting as he points, wins no plaudits from those waiting behind to play.

WHERE AND WHEN
Do not waste time by counting strokes and marking the scorecard just after putting. Putt out, move quickly to the next tee, and record the scores there.

CHAPTER FOUR

TAKING CARE
of the COURSE

WE MUST ALL try to leave the golf
course in a better condition than we find it. If
we don't, then we can't complain when we find
ourselves in an unplayable lie in a bunker because a
fellow player has not bothered to rake his footprints
after playing from the bunker earlier. Leave an
unfilled divot hole one day and the next it might be
your ball that stares at you from below ground.
Putting greens that are bumpy and do
not run true are more often the result of
inconsiderate or lazy golfers than lack of effort
by the greenkeeping staff. When the mark made
by a ball pitching into a green is left without
being repaired immediately, the result is a scar
on the green that can take weeks to heal.
Repaired immediately, the ground will heal
within a matter of hours.

HELP THE GREENKEEPERS
*Your course may not receive the same fastidious
attention as does Augusta National, home of the
Masters, but we all have a duty to support the efforts
of the greenkeeping staff in keeping our course in the
best possible condition.*

REPAIR *the* TEEING GROUND

IN THEORY, FOR TEES where a driving club is used, there should be no divot marks left. The use of a tee should ensure that damage is not done to the turf, but inevitably some players do take divots, even with a driver, and these divots should be replaced.

REPLACE DIVOTS ON THE TEE

It is quite remarkable that some players who act responsibly when it comes to replacing divots on the fairway take no action at all to replace divots taken on the tee.

The tees on short holes get a great deal of harsh treatment, but seldom do we see players replacing often huge pieces of turf removed by their iron tee shots.

REPAIRING DIVOTS

It only takes a few seconds to fill the hole you have made.

The longer-term benefits for the tee are well worth it.

1 *When a divot is taken it should be recovered and replaced immediately after a shot.*

2 *Collect the divot and firmly tamp it down by foot over the exposed patch of earth.*

DON'T PRACTICE SWINGS ON THE TEE

Players who take practice swings carelessly on the tee and remove divots without even playing a shot are the chief offenders.

Always be careful where you take a practice swing.

The only guaranteed way of avoiding unnecessary damage is not to practice swings on the tee at all. If you have to take a practice swing, make certain that you swing the club well clear of the ground.

Filling the hole with sand, or soil-and-grass-seed mix (which helps regenerate the turf), is much better than replacing the turf. Many clubs provide boxes of sand or soil-and-seed on the tees at short holes for this purpose.

And while you are making this repair, carry out this unselfish task: see if you can fill one other hole to compensate for those players who display a lack of consideration (both for the course and for those who have to look after it), when they remove a sizeable piece of real estate and take no steps at all to repair the damage they have caused. By their very nature teeing areas will sustain damage, but some of that damage can be minimized.

Pick Up Broken Tees

Another way to help greenkeeping staff is to pick up your broken tees and deposit them in the trash can beside the tee. Broken tees, particularly if they are made of plastic, can cause damage to mowing machine blades. It's a small point perhaps but one that virtually every golfer ignores. Save the greenkeeping staff time, and help them protect their machinery by collecting your own broken tees.

RUBBISH REMOVAL
Broken tees can be a menace and it doesn't take much effort to collect any you come across while picking up your own tee.

BE A TIDY PLAYER IN ALL SENSES

The same applies to all forms of rubbish. Don't be an untidy golfer. Keep your golf course clean. Put all trash in the cans provided and avoid leaving anything on the ground that could cause damage to machinery.

FAIRWAY REPAIRS

Not all clubs insist you replace divots on the fairway. This depends where in the world you are playing. In the United States, many courses have Bermuda grass in the fairways. A divot of Bermuda grass, once it has been removed, will not grow again when it is replaced, and most clubs with this species of fairway grass prefer that the divots not be replaced. In such circumstances golf carts carry dispensers of sand to fill in the hole left by the divot. The area soon recovers because of the fast-growing and creeping nature of the grass.

In Europe, where golf carts are rare, carrying sand or soil to fill in divot holes is not so practical. When a divot is taken it should be recovered, replaced, and firmly tamped down by foot.

If it is replaced carefully, the turf has a chance to grow again and the hole is not left to provide a potentially bad lie for later players.

BUNKER CARE

BUNKERS ARE DESIGNED as hazards on a golf course, but that does not mean that they should resemble deserts where herds of wild animals have been trampling. It is part of the etiquette of looking after the course to rake over your footprints for the next player.

RAKE'S PROGRESS
Always rake over a bunker once you have played from it.

USE THE BUNKER RAKE PROVIDED

There was a time in the early days of the organized game when bunkers were not raked and players were severely punished if their ball

RAKE AND MAKE GOOD

Always rake a bunker after you have played from it to smooth over the disruption you have caused. If some thoughtless player before you has left footprints elsewhere in the bunker, do the decent thing and rake them over, too.

There is nothing more frustrating than finding your ball resting in someone's footprint.

If a rake is not available, you can use the back of a club to smooth over your footprints.

found the sand. In most cases the modern game offers at least a fair chance of escape from a bunker and the sand is raked regularly to give the player a reasonable chance to play a recovery shot.

Greenkeeping staff look after bunkers, and most clubs provide bunker rakes for players to smooth the sand after they have played a shot.

Sadly, the rakes are not always used, and there is nothing more frustrating for a player first to find his ball in a bunker and then to find that his chances of being able to get it out are severely diminished because the ball is nestling in someone's footprint. This is yet another classic case of golfers not showing consideration for their fellow players.

REPAIRS *on the* GREEN

E VERY PLAYER WANTS smooth greens on which to putt. The main reason they don't always get them is that careless golfers, who are often the first to complain when the greens get bumpy, leave pitch marks and other indentations that they do not attempt to repair.

TAKING CARE OF PITCH MARKS

Pitch marks – the indentations made by golf balls pitching on a green – are the main cause of bumpy greens if they are not properly repaired. Every time a player walks onto a putting green, he should find the mark his ball made when it landed and repair any damage made.

In addition, he should find at least one other pitch mark, and better still two others, that other players have carelessly and thoughtlessly left unattended, and fix those while he is about it.

A pitch mark repaired immediately heals itself within about twenty minutes; one left for a few hours takes weeks for nature to repair.

USE A TEE
If you don't have a pitch-mark repairer, a tee makes a perfectly good substitute.

If you want smooth greens that are a joy to putt on, repair your pitch marks. It is for your own benefit as well as a courtesy to those players coming behind.

PITCH-MARK REPAIRERS

So concerned are they to have pitch marks repaired that many golf courses provide a special tool for repairing pitch marks free of charge to their members or guests.

Always carry a repair tool in your pocket ready for use – and use it! If you forget to take one, a tee can be pressed into service as a useful alternative.

REPAIR TOOL
Always carry the invaluable pitch-mark repairer with you.

REPAIRING PITCH MARKS

Making a point of repairing pitch marks has the added advantage of encouraging others to follow suit. It could even save you several strokes a round if putts go in that might otherwise have been deflected by an unfixed pitch mark.

1 *Repair any marks immediately. The correct method is to push the repair tool into the green around the indentation and push the turf back toward the center to fill the indentation.*

2 *Fill the hollow as much as possible, then tap the surface down gently with the putter to restore the area to a smooth surface. This simple task can save weeks of recovery.*

DON'T LEAN ON YOUR PUTTER

The putter is a vital part of any player's equipment, but it can also cause damage to the green if it is not carefully handled on vulnerable putting surfaces.

In any group of four players on a putting green, it is a safe bet that three of them are leaning on their putters waiting for their turn to putt while the fourth is over the ball. It is a natural thing to do, but if we lean too heavily on the putter the head leaves an indentation in the green; and this might just be the one that deflects your putt the next time you play the hole.

Resting the putter lightly on the ground will not cause any damage. However, it is much more preferable to carry the putter under the arm while waiting your turn to putt.

∇ POSE
TO AVOID
Don't lean on your putter while waiting to putt, as leaning too heavily will leave an indentation on the green.

▷ OUT OF
HARM'S WAY
Always keep the putter off the ground when not in use.

There is a thin line between resting the putter gently on the green, causing no damage, and simply using it as a leaning post.

DON'T USE THE PUTTER AS A LEVER

Another misuse of the putter, which can cause damage to the green in the vital area around the hole, arises when the putter is used as a lever when retrieving the ball from the hole. This practice is common. The player gratefully holes out, bends down to pick the ball from the hole, and uses his putter as a leaning post to lever himself back into an upright position.

The temptation is obvious, but for the next player coming along and facing a short putt, the resulting damage to the area around the hole can be devastating. Players with bad backs are understandably more guilty than others of using the putter as a lever. The comfort of an additional aid to retrieve the ball is often hard to resist.

RETRIEVING THE BALL
Do not use your putter to help yourself back into an upright position after retrieving the ball.

PICKING UP – THE SENSIBLE APPROACH

If you must rest your putter on the ground when retrieving the ball, do so gently with consideration for the green and the players who are following you.

If you need a lever to get you back up from ground level, take the easy option – get hold of one of those very useful rubber cups for the end of the putter shaft. It retrieves the ball from the hole without you even having to bend!

FLAGSTICK ETIQUETTE

The flagstick on a green may seem an innocuous piece of equipment, requiring little attention other than removal from the hole when required and replacement afterward. However, some players are very careless when performing either task, and damage is often done to the hole through simple lack of attention.

WELL OUT OF HARM'S WAY
Ensure you put the flag well away from the hole and from the line of putt of other players.

REMOVING THE FLAGSTICK

When removing the flagstick, the player should make sure that he pulls the flagstick vertically out of its locating hole in the cup, and safely clear of the hole itself, before laying it carefully at the side of the green, well out of the putting line of the other players.

   If the flagstick is carelessly removed, it is very easy to damage the rim of the hole with the bottom of the flagstick.

REPLACING THE FLAGSTICK

Be particularly careful when replacing the flagstick. Carelessness in this action causes the most damage.

Make sure the flagstick is in a vertical position before inserting it into the hole. Damage occurs when the flagstick is inserted at an angle and catches the edge of the hole as it is replaced.

BE CAREFUL WITH SHOE SPIKES

Spikes in golf shoes are an indispensable part of a golfer's equipment. They provide a good foundation for the golf swing and prevent slipping when the course is wet. But spikes can cause a huge amount of damage to putting surfaces if players are not careful how they walk on the green. Tears and scars on the green caused by scuffing feet can easily deflect a putt.

The considerate player always taps down spike marks for the benefit of those coming behind, but only *after he has putted out.* This is perfectly within the Rules (*see page 71*).

CONSIDER PLASTIC SPIKES

Golfers are increasingly moving toward the use of "plastic" spikes. This type of spike is set to replace the conventional sharp steel spike because it appears to cause less damage to the playing surface than the traditional spike.

SPIKE SENSE
Tread with care on soft, wet greens, especially if you have sharp metal spikes; otherwise you can cause damage.

The plastic spike is threaded into the shoe in exactly the same way as the traditional spike. However, instead of being pointed and sharp it features small gripping flanges arranged in a circle on the spike base. Many clubs now insist that all players must wear these new spikes and offer free replacement of traditional spikes for members, guests, and visitors.

You need to weigh the benefits, in terms of reduced damage to greens, against the slight loss of grip in wet conditions. But plastic spikes could still be a step in the right direction.

MOTORIZED CARTS

The wide wheels on motorized carts ensure that in sensible use they will not cause much damage to the golf course. However, if carelessly used, the carts can be a source of damage, particularly when close to the green.

Motorized carts should be kept well clear of greens. Most clubs that have

CART COURTESY
Never take your cart on to tees or putting greens. Always follow course signs directing where to take them.

TAPPING DOWN SPIKE MARKS

Remember that the Rules of Golf do not allow for tapping down spike marks on the line

of a putt. Pitch marks and old hole plugs can be repaired and tapped down flush with the surface of the green. Damage (i.e. spike marks) may be repaired provided it is not on the line of the putt and does not assist in subsequent play of the hole.

REMEMBER THE RULE
Repairing spike damage on the line of a putt carries a two-stroke penalty.

carts mark the point at which they should be driven off the fairway and well away from the green. Restrictions on where carts are allowed to go are made with the best condition of the course in mind, and not simply to frustrate the golfer and make him walk a little farther to his ball.

PULL CARTS

Pull carts should be kept off greens, not because the wheels will cause damage, but because the bottom of the frame, which rests on the ground when the cart is stationary, can easily tear the putting surface.

Pull carts should also be kept clear of the areas between greenside bunkers and the putting surface, since constant walking around these areas compacts the soil, creating poor lies and increased wear and tear.

CHAPTER FIVE

KNOW *the* RULES

WHILE THIS BOOK concentrates on the unwritten rules of the game – the etiquette of common courtesy and sensible time-saving strategies – the golfer must understand the written rules of golf if he is to fully appreciate where and how etiquette comes into play. The intention of this chapter is to outline the basic "ground rules" for all players.

The book of the *Rules of Golf* runs to 146 pages; the book on the *Decisions on the Rules of Golf* runs to several hundred pages more. This represents more regulation and interpretation of the conduct of the game than can be found in any other sporting pastime.

With these rules, the golfer is his own referee and is trusted to be so by his fellow players. This trust is a fundamental part of the game and the single element that sets the game apart from all others.

RULES OFFICIALS FOR THE PROS
Other than in exceptional circumstances – in tournament matches as shown here, for instance – there are no referees to administer the rules during play.

THE RULE BOOK

EVERY PLAYER, WHETHER newcomer or not, should study and become familiar with the Rules of Golf. Only a few know all or even most of the answers, but every player should ensure they have a good working knowledge of those rules that present themselves most often in the course of a round.

READING THE RULES

There is no substitute for reading and understanding the Rules of Golf, but it is a complicated publication. Much of it is devoted to aspects of the game or situations that occur only rarely in a round of golf.

There are certain key rules, however, that surface more frequently than others. In some cases they are misunderstood and regularly misinterpreted as a result.

THE RULES OF GOLF

Every golfer can easily acquire a copy of the Rules of Golf. The books are available at most golf courses and clubs, as well as golf stores. Alternatively, you may obtain a copy for a nominal fee from the

United States Golf Association,
P.O. Box 708,
Far Hills, NJ 07931-0708;
Phone (908) 234-2300 or
Fax (908) 234-2179

CARRY A RULE BOOK *Every golfer should carry a rule book to ensure that reference can be made to it if a question presents itself during play. It is a compact journal that fits easily into a golf bag.*

There are, broadly, eight headings under which the rules most widely encountered by the average player are contained. They are in effect the "working" rules of the game.

These fundamental rules cover:

1. **Playing the ball as it lies.**
2. **Searching for and identifying the ball.**
3. **Dealing with an unplayable ball.**
4. **Dealing with a lost ball.**
5. **Dealing with a ball out of bounds.**
6. **Dealing with water hazards.**
7. **Dealing with loose impediments and obstructions.**
8. **Local Rules.**

But within these headings lie many different situations that you are bound to encounter.

ASPECTS *of* PLAY

THE NEXT FEW PAGES analyze some of the rules governing seven of the most important aspects of the game of golf. Ultimately, it is better to have practical grasp of these key aspects than it is to try to learn all the rules. This section is followed by a look at how Local Rules can influence play.

ASPECTS OF PLAY 1

PLAYING THE BALL AS IT LIES

This is a fundamental aspect of the game and yet the Rules of Golf do not make any mention of it until Rule 13-1, which states that "the ball must be played as it lies, except as otherwise provided in the Rules."

In days gone by, golfers carried strange implements such as water irons with holes in the face to play from water, or rut irons with small heads to play from the rutted tracks left by carts.

Today's game is not quite so hidebound. A player is not forced to play from water and only from a rut when it is not declared Ground Under Repair (GUR).

LATERAL HAZARD
The red posts indicate that, although dry, this is a lateral water hazard. In this instance, Jose Maria Olazabal opted to play the ball as it lay.

DON'T TOUCH!

Essentially the player should play the ball as he finds it. He has the right to mark and clean the ball on the putting green but otherwise there is no need to touch it, or move it, from the time he tees it up until when he retrieves it from the hole.

SPRINKLER HEAD
Local Rules allow for a free drop from such local obstructions.

DROPPING FROM WATER
If the ball lies in a water hazard, as shown left, you may drop under penalty of one stroke. The Rules now allow a free drop from water, if it is casual water such as a rain-filled puddle (Rule 25-1b), or a drop under penalty of one stroke if the ball lies in a water hazard, such as a lake or brook (Rule 26-1).

ASPECTS OF PLAY 2

SEARCHING FOR AND IDENTIFYING THE BALL

IDENTIFYING A BALL
You can remove grass, leaves, or mud solely to identify a ball if not in a hazard.

It is one of the paradoxes of golf that a player is not necessarily entitled to see his ball when playing a stroke. When conducting a search for his ball anywhere on the course, the player is allowed to move only grass, mud, and the like, to the extent that doing so allows him to find the ball and identify it as his. He must

Mark Your Ball

The responsibility for playing the correct ball rests with the player (Rule 12-2). To avoid confusion, put an identifying mark on your ball using indelible ink. A pattern of dots or your own initials serves well. A manufacturer's name and number are simply not sufficient to guard against misidentification.

MARK YOUR BALL
Use an indelible marker to identify your ball.

not, in the course of the search, improve the lie of the ball, the area of his intended swing, or the line of play. In any situation on the course *except in a hazard* the player is allowed, however, to lift a ball he believes to be his own, without penalty, for the purposes of identification.

He can clean the ball to the extent necessary to confirm that it is his, but he *must* inform his opponent or fellow competitor of his intention to do so, to allow an opportunity to have his actions observed. He must mark the position of the ball and replace it correctly after identification. A player who fails to comply with these requirements is in breach of Rule 20-3a, which carries a penalty of one stroke. The ball is then replaced.

ASPECTS OF PLAY 3

DEALING WITH AN UNPLAYABLE BALL

YOU DECIDE
It is up to you to decide if your ball is unplayable. You are the sole referee.

From time to time, every player in the course of his career will find his ball in a position from which he cannot play it. The player has sole discretion in deciding if a ball is playable or not. Having declared it unplayable, he has three options:

DROPPING THE BALL

The player is the sole judge of when a ball is unplayable, but the rules are strict on how to drop the ball correctly after it has been declared unplayable by the player.

1 *Measure two club lengths from where the ball lies.*

2 *Drop the ball at arm's length and shoulder height within two club lengths of where the ball lay, but not nearer the hole.*

(a) he may return to the spot from which the ball was last played;

(b) he may drop the ball within two club-lengths of where the ball lay, but not nearer the hole;

(c) he may drop the ball as far behind the point where the ball lay as he wishes, provided he keeps that point on a line directly between the hole and the spot on which he then drops the ball.

The penalty for breach of Rule 28 is loss of the hole in match play and a two-stroke penalty in stroke play.

UNPLAYABLE IN A BUNKER

If the ball is declared unplayable in a bunker, the same options apply, except that the ball has to be dropped in the bunker, unless the player opts to return to the spot from which the ball was originally played and play again.

ASPECTS OF PLAY 4

DEALING WITH A LOST BALL

Rule 27, which deals with a ball lost or out of bounds, is probably the rule the golfer comes up against most often. The procedure, however, is quite straightforward when fully understood.

FIVE-MINUTE RULE
You are allowed five minutes to search for a lost ball. Play a provisional ball to save time if the original ball is not found within the time limit.

If a ball is lost, the player must play another ball from as near as possible to the point from which the original ball was played, and add one stroke to his score. The penalty for a lost ball is therefore loss of a stroke and the distance the lost ball covered, that is, stroke and distance.

If a player suspects that he will not find his

ball, he should immediately declare his intention to play a "provisional" ball, that is, one which will replace the original ball if it is not found. A player is entitled to search for his ball for five minutes after which, if it is not found, he must put another ball in play.

He must either return to the spot from which he originally played and put another ball in play from that spot, or, if that spot was on the tee, he is entitled to tee the replacement ball.

If he has played a provisional ball, he must then proceed with that ball as the ball in play.

SAVING TIME

There is no penalty for playing a provisional ball if the original ball is found – and it saves time on the course if the original ball is lost.

ASPECTS OF PLAY 5

DEALING WITH A BALL
OUT OF BOUNDS

A ball out of bounds, that is, beyond the
boundary of the course, is dealt with in the
same way as a lost ball. If a player suspects his
ball is out of bounds, he should immediately
play a provisional ball, as in a suspected lost
ball situation, and proceed in the same way.

If he does not play a provisional ball, and
subsequently establishes that his ball is out of
bounds, he must return to the point from
where the ball was originally played and put
another ball in play from that spot.

The penalty is exactly the same, that is,
stroke and distance, as it is for a ball lost.

SHOT INTO ROUGH
*Ball is driven into deep rough from the
tee and not found within five minutes.*

PROVISIONAL BALL
*Provisional ball is played to save time
in case original ball is not found.*

UNDERSTANDING STROKE AND DISTANCE

There is sometimes confusion over how many strokes a player has taken under the stroke and distance penalty. The following examples explain the penalty:

1 A player drives his ball into deep rough from the tee and fails to find it within the five-minute period.

3 He is then playing his third shot from the spot where he played his original ball – "three from tee."

2 He must therefore return to the tee and put another ball in play.

1 A player plays his second shot into deep rough and suspects that he will not find it.

3 His next stroke is therefore his fifth under the stroke and distance penalty.

2 He then plays a provisional ball to save time in case he does not find it. As feared, he fails to find the original ball and continues with the provisional ball, which becomes the ball in play.

ASPECTS OF PLAY 6

DEALING WITH WATER HAZARDS

Water hazards, dealt with under Rule 26, probably account for more penalty shots in the career of a golfer than anything else. They are often a source of controversy when it comes to interpretation of the rules.

WHAT IS A WATER HAZARD?

Many players are confused by the belief that there are two types of water hazard, when in fact this is not the case.

The Rules of Golf define a water hazard as "any sea, lake, pond, river, ditch, surface draining ditch or other open water course (whether or not containing water), and anything of a similar nature." Water hazards are marked on the course by yellow stakes or lines. But, in addition (and this is where the confusion arises), the Rules make provision for a part of a water hazard to be defined as a "lateral water hazard" – a part of a water hazard "so situated that it is not deemed possible by the Committee to drop a ball behind the water hazard in accordance with Rule 26-1b."

IS IT LATERAL?
Check if the water hazard is a lateral one with red markers, or a normal hazard with yellow markers.

In effect, this means a water hazard that does not lie between the player and the green. A lateral water hazard should be clearly marked with red stakes or lines.

WHAT TO DO IN WATER

The procedures for dealing with a ball which lies in, is lost in, or touches a water hazard are as follows:

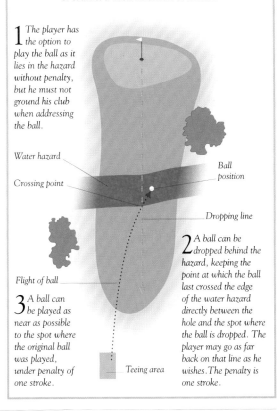

1 The player has the option to play the ball as it lies in the hazard without penalty, but he must not ground his club when addressing the ball.

Water hazard

Crossing point

Ball position

Dropping line

2 A ball can be dropped behind the hazard, keeping the point at which the ball last crossed the edge of the water hazard directly between the hole and the spot where the ball is dropped. The player may go as far back on that line as he wishes. The penalty is one stroke.

Flight of ball

3 A ball can be played as near as possible to the spot where the original ball was played, under penalty of one stroke.

Teeing area

LATERAL WATER HAZARD

If the ball lands in an area designated as a lateral water
hazard, the player has a further option.

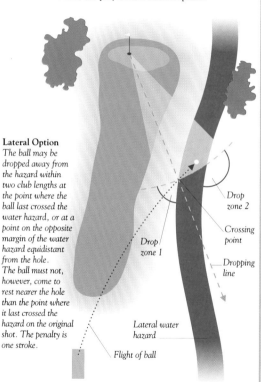

Lateral Option
*The ball may be
dropped away from
the hazard within
two club lengths at
the point where the
ball last crossed the
water hazard, or at a
point on the opposite
margin of the water
hazard equidistant
from the hole.
The ball must not,
however, come to
rest nearer the hole
than the point where
it last crossed the
hazard on the original
shot. The penalty is
one stroke.*

Drop
zone 2

Crossing
point

Dropping
line

Drop
zone 1

Lateral water
hazard

Flight of ball

LOCATING THE PLACE TO PLAY

Be careful to establish the point at which the ball last *crossed* the margin of the water hazard. It is essential to determine this spot as it dictates from where you will measure your drop. This is where confusion most commonly arises.

Best advice is to go to the point where the ball was last on, or over, dry land before it crossed into the water. Establish whether that point is within an area of yellow or red lines or stakes and proceed from there, referring to the illustrations on pages 87 and 88.

BALL LOST IN A WATER HAZARD

In order to treat a ball as lost in a hazard, there must be "reasonable evidence" that the ball lodged in it. An audible or visible splash of water is usually enough to indicate that it is lost inside a water hazard, although this is not always the case (Decision 26-1/1). In the absence of such evidence, the ball must be treated as a lost ball (*see pages 82 and 83*). If in doubt as to whether it is a water or lateral water hazard, go to the point where the ball crossed and look for identifying red or yellow markers.

PLAY OPTIONS
You can play another shot from the tee, or drop a ball behind the edge of the water. Identify where the original ball last crossed the margin of the water hazard: this spot must lie directly between where you drop the ball and the hole. The penalty is one stroke.

ASPECTS OF PLAY 7

DEALING WITH LOOSE IMPEDIMENTS AND OBSTRUCTIONS

There are many objects that come under the heading of "Loose Impediments" or "Obstructions" that can interfere with a player's ball, stance, or swing. Rules 23 and 24 deal with loose impediments and obstructions. The rules are intricate and should be studied carefully.

Loose impediments are defined in the Rules as "natural objects such as stones, leaves, twigs, branches and the like, dung, worms and insects and casts or heaps made by them, provided

THE BRUSH OFF
Loose bunker sand may only be brushed off the green.

they are not fixed or growing, are solidly embedded and do not adhere to the ball."

Obstructions are anything artificial, such as artificial surfaces and sides of roads and paths and other manmade objects such as, for instance, manufactured ice.

For the most part the player is entitled to relief from obstructions and to remove loose impediments without penalty, but there are one or two traps for the unwary.

WHAT ARE LOOSE IMPEDIMENTS?

Sand and loose soil, for instance, are loose impediments only on the green. A player who moves sand or soil on the fringe of the

BALL IN A BOTTLE

If the ball lies in or on a movable obstruction, the ball may be lifted without penalty and the obstruction removed. The ball is then replaced as near as possible to the spot where it lay in or on the obstruction. This is the rule that would have given Irishman Harry Bradshaw relief in the famous "ball in the bottle" incident in the Open Championship at Royal St. Georges in 1949. Bradshaw's drive finished inside half a broken bottle. He was not sure whether he was entitled to relief and played the ball while it was still in the bottle. He was of course entitled to relief and went on to lose a playoff against Bobby Locke.

IS IT LOOSE?
Provided that natural objects, such as leaves, pine needles, and insects are not fixed or growing, you may remove them from around the ball. But you must not cause the ball to be moved in the process.

green is in breach of Rule 23-1, the penalty for which is loss of hole in match play and two strokes in stroke play.

Don't brush away dew or frost from around your ball; neither are loose impediments. However, snow and natural ice can be treated either as casual water, in which case the ball can be dropped without penalty at the nearest point of relief not nearer the hole, or as loose impediments, in which case they can be removed.

Be particularly careful when removing loose impediments anywhere within a club length of the ball. If the ball moves, the player is deemed to have moved it and he incurs a one-stroke penalty. The ball must then be replaced.

If a player's ball lies in, or on, an immovable obstruction, or is so close to it that the obstruction interferes with his stance or intended swing, the player is entitled to lift his ball and drop it at the nearest point of relief.

A player is not entitled to relief from an immovable obstruction if the ball is in a water hazard, including a lateral water hazard. If an obstruction is a movable one, such as a post marking a water hazard or a bunker rake, the obstruction can be moved. If the ball moves there is no penalty, but it must be replaced.

BUNKER OBSTRUCTION
If the ball comes to rest against a bunker rake, the rake may be moved. There is no penalty if the ball moves while you do this, but the ball must be replaced in its original position.

LOCAL RULES

PLAYERS SHOULD ALWAYS check Local Rules. These will cover abnormal conditions on the course, the status of obstructions, stones in bunkers, unusual damage on the course, temporary obstructions, preferred lies, winter rules, and environmentally sensitive areas.

DON'T MAKE ASSUMPTIONS

Never assume that, because one golf club makes a Local Rule allowing stones in bunkers to be treated as movable obstructions, all clubs will do the same.

Some clubs make roads and paths or shelters integral parts of the course, which means that there is no relief from them if they interfere with a player's ball, stroke, or stance. The ball in such circumstances must be played as it lies.

GOLF COURSE BULLETIN BOARD

Local Rules will be posted on the course bulletin board and, except for those of limited duration, printed on the club's scorecard. It is always a good idea to check the bulletin board and the scorecard for Local Rules before going out to play first time on a course. For example, you might assume that relief from fixed sprinkler heads is normally provided for under a Local Rule, but it may not be. It's always best to check first.

OFFICIAL RULINGS

Consulting an official of the course (assuming one is immediately available), and asking for a ruling, is not always feasible when a complex decision on the Rules arises during a round, particularly in a competition, and there is doubt or dispute as to how to proceed.

The best way around the problem is to play out the hole in question with two balls to cover the options in dispute, and seek a decision on the rule as soon as possible at the end of the round. The Committee will decide which ball should count for the final score, and whether any penalties apply. However, two balls can be played only in stroke-play events (Rule 3-3).

PLAY TWO
If in doubt about how a rule applies to your particular situation, in the interests of saving time on the course, play out the hole with two balls to cover the options in dispute. Then settle it later.

SCORING *in* COMPETITION

GOLF IS THE ONLY sport in which official scores are recorded by a fellow competitor. That player is responsible for the correctness of the score on every hole. At the end of a round, double-check that your marker has not filled in your score incorrectly.

STROKE-PLAY RESPONSIBILITY

In a stroke-play competition, a player must assume the responsibility of marking a fellow competitor's scorecard. The marker must remember three things: to assess how many strokes the competitor takes to complete the hole; to check how many strokes were taken; and to record the score on the card.

The marker is *not* responsible for adding the scores on the scorecard. That task is reserved for the Committee once the scorecards are handed in.

WRITE THE CORRECT SCORE

Players must also ensure that their correct handicaps have been recorded on the scorecards. Remember, innocent mistakes do happen. Players are entirely responsible for making sure that their correct scores are added to their own cards for each hole. The scores for which they sign at the end of the round cannot be changed.

- *If a player signs for a score at one hole that is one stroke more than he took for the hole, that score must count.*

- *If a player signs for a score at one hole that is one less than he actually took, then he will be disqualified.*

In one famous incident, the Argentinian Roberto de Vicenzo lost the chance of a playoff against Bob Goalby in the 1968 Masters when he signed for a 4 at the 17th hole, instead of the birdie 3 he had scored. The score had to stand despite the fact that it was clearly a clerical error.

YOUR SCORECARD

Not only is the scorecard a record of your score, it is also a source of valuable information about the course, such as distances and Local Rules.

TEE LENGTHS
Most courses have a selection of tees

HOLE LENGTH
Lengths as measured from the various tees

STROKE INDEX
Holes at which allocated strokes must be taken

SCORE RECORD
Column for score

POINTS RECORD
Column for recording points if playing under a points system

SIGNATURES
Both player and marker must sign for card to be valid

MARKER	PARTNER	H	YARDS		YARDS	STROKE INDEX	A	PTS.	B	PTS.	YARDS		STROKE INDEX
		1	524	5	504	5	15				451	5	13
		2	365	4	355	4	11				336	4	5
		3	426	4	414	4	1				396	4	3
		4	195	3	170	3	5				165	3	15
		5	444	4	432	4	7				414	4	11
		6	391	4	376	4	9				361	4	1
		7	137	3	135	3	17				137	3	17
		8	548	5	536	5	13				416	5	9
		9	413	4	360	4	3				353	4	7
			3443	36	3320	36	TOTAL OUT						
		10	317	4	300	4	8				292	4	10
		11	500	5	485	5	14				468	5	6
		12	414	4	399	4	4				376	4	4
		13	139	3	130	3	18				122	3	18
		14	381	4	362	4	10				350	4	2
		15	403	4	386	4	2				376	4	12
		16	346	4	341	4	16				312	4	16
		17	165	3	160	3	6				149	3	14
		18	362	4	360	4	12				332	4	8
			3027	35	2921	35	TOTAL IN						
			3443	36	3320	36	TOTAL OUT						
			6470	71	6241	71	TOTAL						
							H/CAP						
							NETT						

COMPETITION
TEE S.S.S. DATE
WHITE 72 71 **PLAYER A.** H/CAP STROKES RECEIVED.
YELLOW 72 70 **PLAYER B.**
RED 73 73

MARKER'S SIGNATURE

PLAYER'S SIGNATURE

DECISIONS *on the* RULES

THE RULES OF GOLF are complicated. Those who make them have tried to keep them as simple as possible, but confusion and disputes over interpretation inevitably occur. Avoid altercations, and seek a decision from the Committee.

FINAL DECISIONS

In the absence of a referee, a dispute over the Rules should be referred to the Committee of the club, whose decision should be final. In circumstances where the Committee cannot come to a decision, it should refer the dispute or doubtful point to the Rules of Golf Committee of the USGA or the R&A in St. Andrews, whose decision shall be final.

However, if a dispute or doubtful point over the Rules has not been referred to the Rules of Golf Committee for an opinion, any player has the right to seek clarification from the Rules of Golf Committee.

REFERRALS

The player can refer an agreed statement on the dispute, through the golf professional of his course, to the Rules of Golf Committee for an opinion on the correctness of any decision given. The reply will be sent to the professional concerned, but players should not approach the Rules of Golf Committee directly for an opinion. All inquiries must be sent through the golf club professional.

USEFUL PUBLICATION

A very useful book entitled *Decisions on the Rules of Golf* (published by the R&A and the USGA) has the answers to a thousand questions on the Rules, and is an invaluable reference book for all serious golfers.

It is available from either:
The United States Golf Association,
P.O. Box 708, Far Hills, NJ 07931-0708; or
The Royal & Ancient Golf Club of
St. Andrews, Fife, KY16 9JD, Scotland.

ON-THE-SPOT RULING
The Rules apply to all golfers – professionals have to consult the rule book, too, and sometimes even they have to get a ruling from a tournament referee.

CHAPTER SIX

PLAYING AWAY *from* HOME

NEW GOLFERS OFTEN FIND it difficult to obtain
practical "need-to-know" information such as how
to book tee times at other courses, how to obtain a
letter of introduction to another club, how to
report scores from an away-from-home
competition, or what may be needed for
the golfer traveling overseas.

Experienced players always carry a handicap card
with them whenever they play away from their
home club; and they have learned, often through
painful experience, how to protect their golf clubs
adequately when traveling. But the game has no
clearinghouse for this information, and this
chapter aims to provide the most essential points.

RESEARCH THE NEW PATCH
*Always check what special Local Rules apply at the club
you are visiting. They will be posted in the clubhouse or
pro shop, and printed on the course card.*

VISITING *a* NEW COURSE

THE GROWING POPULARITY of golf puts ever-increasing pressure on tee times. The chances of turning up unannounced at a golf club and hoping to get an immediate game are slim indeed. Some advanced planning is required.

HOW TO BOOK TEE TIMES

Many public courses require advance starting times, especially at weekends, and even among the private clubs there are few that do not now operate a starting time system. The exceptions are mainly small, remote clubs with relatively small memberships and few casual visitors. Elsewhere, booking tee times in advance is essential.

Normal procedure is simply to call the pro shop and ask which

VALDERRAMA
The more famous the golf resort, the more likely that advanced booking is essential.

times are available. Times can usually be booked days or even weeks ahead, but there are a few courses that will assign times only a day in advance.

Many of the most famous or most popular clubs require considerable advance notice.

PLAYING AT ST. ANDREWS

A most famous example is the Old Course at St. Andrews. The pressure on advance tee times is so great at the Home of Golf that the percentage of tee times available for pre-booking well in advance is taken up as soon as the tee times become available at the beginning of October each year.

In practice, most visitors to this famous links need to apply through the daily ballot system, which requires them to apply for times at the Links Management offices before 2pm for the following day's play. Naturally, this can be done by telephone.

ST. ANDREWS
Golf has been played at St. Andrews for more than 400 years, and everyone wants to play on the hallowed Old Course. If you don't get a time in the ballot, do not give up hope. Speak to the starter; gaps need to be filled occasionally.

BOOKING IN ADVANCE

Most clubs will accept applications for tee times over the telephone. However, the best approach often is to write personally to the golf professional with your request.

It is also worthwhile to ask in your letter if the dates you have requested are likely to clash with any major work being undertaken on the course. There is nothing more frustrating than to book a tee time well in advance and arrive at the course for a keenly awaited game, only to find the greenkeeping staff aerating or top-dressing the greens.

Most clubs now know what their maintenance schedules are likely to be well in advance.

LANDOR GOLF CLUB
CERTIFICATE OF HANDICAP

Mr/Ms .... is

a member of the
Landor Golf Club

His/her Present Handicap is
.... Strokes.

....
GOLF PROFESSIONAL

The Course Rating is 71

CERTIFIED
Your initial handicap is calculated from the average score of three games on the same course.

CARRY A HANDICAP CERTIFICATE

Always carry a handicap card when visiting golf clubs away from home. Many clubs will not allow visitors to play without production of a handicap card; others make it a condition of being able to play on the course, even though they do not demand to see it.

The best advice is always to carry one. Not only does a handicap card establish you as a golfer, it also verifies that you are a member of a golf club or established course.

CARRY A LETTER OF INTRODUCTION

A letter of introduction from your own golf professional may also save you time and frustration when seeking to play other courses. It takes only a few minutes of the pro's time to write a letter confirming that you are a legitimate golfer and introducing you to the professional of any other club you visit.

Armed with such a document, your chances of obtaining a tee time at even the most exclusive golf club or course are considerably enhanced, and such a letter will stand you in good stead and remain current for a considerable length of time.

BOOKING A TEE TIME

Your letter should include:

- *Your home club if you have one.*

- *Your current handicap, preferably with a confirmation from your own club professional.*

- *The date and time when you wish to play, with alternatives if your original choice is not available.*

- *Whether you require meals during your visit.*

- *How many will be in your party.*

Details of the other players' handicaps and course affiliations should also be included. Ask for confirmation in writing of the times you have been allocated, and of the green fees that will apply during your visit.

THE PLAYER WITHOUT A CLUB

The great golf boom of the 1980s and 1990s has resulted in many more golfers taking up the game than there are club membership places available for them. Without club membership these players cannot obtain an official handicap, and without an official handicap many clubs will not accept them for membership anyway. It is a classic Catch-22 situation.

It is also a situation that creates particular problems for newcomers or inexperienced players who want to play at courses that will allow only visitors who have an official handicap. There is, unfortunately, no easy answer to this dilemma.

However, there are a few things that the newcomer without a handicap can do to counteract the difficulties. Investing in lessons with a golf pro offers the best chance of breaking down some of the barriers put in the player-without-a-handicap's way. In any event, it is the best way to learn the basics of golf.

NEWCOMER TO OLD COURSE
The best way to avoid lines is to make the right kind of approach to golf professionals when seeking to book a tee time.

RESPECT THE RULES

When visiting another course, remember to respect the rules and standards that the course has set out on its bulletin board and scorecard. It must never be overlooked that visitors to golf courses are invited guests and as such owe a duty to their hosts and to the integrity of the game.

INVEST IN LESSONS

Invest in lessons from a qualified PGA professional. The professional can judge when a player is competent to move from the practice area to the golf course.

- *A club's teaching professional will give lessons to anyone, whether or not they are members at his club.*
- *Ask the professional for a letter of confirmation that lessons have been taken, together with an assessment of your current ability.*

- *Learn the essential rules and etiquette and make a point of informing the professional at the course you wish to play, or in a letter requesting a tee time, that you understand them.*
- *Include a copy of your professional's assessment with your letter.*

REPORTING SCORES

A GOLFER HAS RESPONSIBILITIES both to himself and to his fellow players to insure that the handicapping system under which he plays operates effectively and in equity. Conscientious scoring is therefore a part of the overall etiquette of the game.

YOUR DUTY TO REPORT

The different handicapping systems that operate around the world have one thing in common: scores need to be reported to a player's home club if the handicapping system is to operate effectively and efficiently.

HANDICAPS LOGGED ON COMPUTER

In the United States, handicapping for both men and women comes under the jurisdiction of the USGA, and a national computer system makes life a little easier. Clubs are linked to a national computer that calculates and keeps track of handicaps. Players simply log in their own scores, together with information on the course they have just played, and the computer does the rest.

In Britain, the National Council of Golf Unions has jurisdiction over the handicapping system, but delegates the operation of the scheme to its affiliated clubs. In Europe, the Golf Unions affiliated to the European Golf Association also operate this same scheme.

Any player who is a member of a club affiliated to one of these organizations is duty-bound to ensure that any scores returned in a qualifying competition away from his home club are reported so that adjustments can be made to his handicap.

In Europe, ladies' golf operates a different handicapping system, although the process is largely the same as for men. The Ladies Golf Union in Britain administers the system, and it is incumbent on each and every player to return scores to their home clubs.

WHAT TO WRITE DOWN

A simple card or letter with the following information should be sent *immediately* to the golf professional after a competition round played away from the player's home course:

Player's Name: ....

Home Club: ....

Handicap (exact): ....

Handicap (playing): ....

Competition: ....

Date: .... CSS: ....

Remember to include:

• *The date and venue of the competition.*

• *The competition scratch score (CSS). It is the player's responsibility to establish what the CSS of the day was.*

• *The gross score returned (stroke-play competition); number of points scored (Stableford competition); the par of the course and the score versus par (par competition).*

TRAVELING ABROAD

A LMOST EVERY DAY, airport carousels around the
world disgorge badly packed golf bags from which
hang bent or broken shafts. This occurrence is
guaranteed to put the damper on any golfing vacation.
However, a few simple precautions may be taken.

PROTECT YOUR CLUBS IN TRANSIT

Follow these steps for packing your bag and
your favorite clubs will be protected from the
baggage handlers.

1 *In transit, store the
clubs with the heads
inside the bag and the
handles to the top. This
is the safest method of
transportation and
prevents the heads
from being
snapped off.*

2 *Remember always to
attach the rain cover
onto the bag as additional
protection for the clubs
before packing the bag
in its own cover.*

3 Invest in a sturdy cover for your golf bag. Although it may provide the best protection, a rigid case made of fiberglass weighs a little more than a tough fabric alternative.

4 Always padlock the cover for security. Golf equipment makes an attractive target for nimble fingers and can be expensive to replace, particularly in some countries.

Clearly mark your destination address

Secure with a padlock

5 Always make sure that your bag and the cover are properly identified with labels.

PLAYING *in* HOT WEATHER

THERE ARE ONE OR TWO essentials that the golfer should ensure are in the golf bag when traveling abroad. If you are leaving to play in warmer climes, make sure you pack wisely and include the items shown here.

INSECT REPELLENT
Mosquitoes love golf courses, particularly if there is an abundance of water.

Sunscreen lotion

SUNSCREEN
There is a growing awareness of the danger of over-exposure to the sun. Vacationing golfers are just as susceptible as sun worshipers. Make sure exposed areas of your skin are protected by a high-factor sunscreen.

Sunblock

WATER BOTTLE
Dehydration is a very real danger for a golfer out in the hot sun for several hours. Carry plenty of water, and drink frequently.

SUNGLASSES
Sensible anti-glare glasses, or sports sun visors, are useful in bright conditions.

LOOK AFTER YOURSELF

"Be prepared" is a maxim often forgotten. It is always useful to have a simple first-aid kit handy, especially when abroad. Infected food can play havoc with your digestion. Tablets for upset stomachs are a sensible addition to the golf bag to counter any ill effects. Antihistamine is also a good idea if you suffer from allergies. Add some antiseptic cream and a few adhesive bandages and keep them in your golf bag.

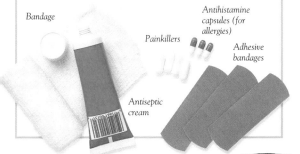

Bandage

Antihistamine capsules (for allergies)

Painkillers

Adhesive bandages

Antiseptic cream

SUN HAT
It can get very hot on most of the golf courses in sunny climes, even in the winter months. A sun hat is certainly advisable.

PLAYING *in* COLD WEATHER

F OR GOLFERS VISITING more temperate climes, the need for sunscreen and water bottles is not generally so pressing, although the sun's rays are still a hazard, as is dehydration. The emphasis should be on keeping totally dry, warm, and comfortable.

WARM HAT
Carry a knit hat or warm cap. It's a vital piece of equipment when the weather turns cold and wet. It keeps body heat in as well as providing cover.

WARM SWEATER
A vital part of any visitor's golf bag accessories. Depending on the time of year, some golf courses can experience all four seasons in sequence, not only in the course of a single day but in the course of a round, so be prepared.

RAIN JACKET
Modern waterproofs are highly flexible and of breathable fabric that allows perspiration to evaporate. It is worth investing in a good-quality jacket and rainpants. But remember, always hang them up to dry after play.

UMBRELLA
Don't leave the umbrella out of the bag just because the sun is shining when you go to the first tee. And buy a good one.

TOWELS
Tie one to the bag and keep an extra towel inside the golf bag to dry off grips if the weather turns nasty.

BAGGAGE CHARGES

THERE IS NO HARD and fast rule among airlines over carrying golf clubs. Some allow golf clubs to be carried free, while others include a golf bag as part of the overall baggage allowance. Again, a telephone call can lead to worthwhile savings and save hassle.

CHECK IN ADVANCE

PEACE OF MIND
Always check with your travel agent for special requirements for any country you plan to visit to play golf.

It is impossible to get a satisfactory answer from airlines as to why there should be such different policies among them concerning golf clubs. Doubtless, some airlines view them as a source of extra income.

The golfer can strike a blow for himself and his fellow golfers by checking in advance with

the airline whether golf clubs are carried free of charge. If an airline refuses to carry them free, take your business to another airline, and explain your choice to the one you reject.

In addition, charter flights to popular warm-weather golf holiday destinations usually have no restrictions on golf club carriage.

PREPARING FOR LONG-HAUL GOLF

Traveling golfers are subject to the same rules as any other travelers when it comes to visas and inoculations for certain countries.

Always make sure you have adequate travel insurance. If you travel abroad several times a year to play golf, an annual travel insurance policy may well be more economical than individual policies for each trip.

GLOSSARY

Professional and amateur golfers alike use a form of "golf-speak" that contains a great many technical terms and colloquial references. The following pages explain a variety of the terms that you are likely to hear in use by playing partners or competitors in the course of a round of golf. The words and phrases clarified here are also likely to make many appearances in the post-round discussion at the clubhouse!

MASTERING THE ESSENTIALS
At the Masters in Augusta, Georgia, spectators getting pairing sheets will see a message from founder Bobby Jones: "In golf, customs of etiquette and decorum are just as important as rules governing play."

GLOSSARY

ADVICE

This is defined as "any counsel or suggestion that could influence a player in determining his play, the choice of club or the method of making a stroke." This means that you can ask for information on matters such as where the flag is situated on the green, or how far it is from a sprinkler head to the center of the green. But you cannot ask anyone other than your playing partner or caddie the distance from your ball to the flag. Be careful about giving advice, too. If you suggest to your fellow competitor in medal play that he might be gripping the club a little tightly, you can be penalized two strokes, even though your intentions were friendly.

BERMUDA GRASS

A strain of grass common in the United States, characterized by thick, wiry leaves and exceptionally clinging roots.

CASUAL WATER

This is any temporary accumulation of water on the course. If there's a puddle by your ball, or even the slightest sign of surface water, you are entitled to relief without penalty.

CLUB COMMITTEE

An elected group of club members responsible for Local Rules, all decisions at club level, and tournament administration.

COMPETITOR AND FELLOW COMPETITOR

A competitor is a player in a stroke competition. A fellow competitor is any person with whom the competitor plays. Neither is a partner of the other. The term only applies in foursomes and fourball competitions.

COMPETITION SCRATCH SCORE (CSS)

This is a figure based on the Standard Scratch Score (SSS) of the course, adjusted

CASUAL WATER, *such as puddles, entitles you to one club-length's relief.*

according to the average score of all competitors playing that day. It therefore takes into account the difficulty of the playing conditions and, as such, is a more accurate way of applying handicaps than the basic SSS. For instance, on a day of driving wind and rain the CSS will be higher than the SSS, reflecting the fact that it is far more difficult for golfers to play to their handicap in such conditions. This figure is generally used more in Great Britain and Europe.

DIVOT
A divot describes the piece of turf and soil dislodged in the process of striking the ball. A divot should always be replaced and tamped down firmly in its original position.

DRESS CODE
Specific rules relating to acceptable attire on the golf course and in the clubhouse.

FIVE MINUTES
That's how long you've got to search for a ball. If your time is up and you still can't locate it, you have to declare the ball lost and proceed in accordance with Rule 27.

FORE
The warning cry or shout a golfer should give at the top of his voice well before the moment his ball might hit another golfer.

FOURBALL
Match involving four players in teams of two, in which each player plays his own ball.

FOURSOME
Match involving four players in teams of two, in which each team plays one ball by alternate strokes. At the start of play each team decides which player will tee-off, after which they alternate the tee-shot on each hole.

FREE DROP
Relief from a condition which carries no penalty – for instance, a player may be allowed a free drop away from a young sapling to avoid damaging the tree. The player is also entitled to a free drop from areas that have been declared ground under repair.

GREEN
An area of closely mown grass specially prepared for putting, into which is cut the hole. It is separated from the fairway by a fringe of grass called the "apron."

GROSS SCORE
This term describes the number of strokes taken, without taking handicaps into account.

GROUND UNDER REPAIR (GUR)
Any portion of the course so marked, usually by stakes or lines painted on the ground. GUR includes material piled for removal or a drainage hole made by the greenkeeper.

HANDICAP CARD
Many clubs insist that visiting golfers bring along a card as proof that they are a member of a club and that they have a proper handicap. Handicap cards are generally issued by the golf professional.

HAZARD
Any bunker or water hazard.

HOLE PLUGS
Imperfections in the green where a previous hole has been filled. If on the line of play, these can be tapped down so that the plug sits more flush with the putting surface.

HOLLOW TINING OR AERATING
This is maintenance work carried out by the greenkeeper, whereby narrow holes are punched into the

putting surface. It is usually carried out around fall and, although the results can look ugly and severe, it forms an integral part of the upkeep of the greens.

HONOR

Having the "honor" entitles a player to tee off first in a group. It is usually determined by the golfer with the lowest score on the previous hole. On the first tee, where there is obviously no previous score to go by, the honor is decided either by handicap order (lowest handicap usually tees off first) or the flip of a coin.

LOCAL RULES

These are rules that are laid down by the Club Committee rather than being set in stone by the R&A or USGA. They usually encompass scenarios and features that are unique to that particular golf course. Because they are not necessarily covered in the Rules of Golf, these local rules are printed on the back of the scorecard of the course and often pinned on the bulletin board in the clubhouse. For visiting golfers playing in a competition, it is always wise to check these rules before going out to play.

LOOSE IMPEDIMENTS

These are natural objects, such as stones, twigs, and worm casts. Generally speaking, although there are exceptions, you are entitled to remove loose impediments if they interfere with play.

MARKED AND LIFTED

Correct procedure for marking a ball on the putting green.

MOVED

It may seem obvious, but there's a perilously thin line between a ball that has moved and one that hasn't. Under the Rules a ball must actually leave its original and come to rest in another place for there to be a penalty applied. So if, say, you are preparing to putt and the putter head touches the ball, there isn't a problem providing the ball doesn't actually leave its original spot.

OBSTRUCTIONS *are anything artificial and could include this cart.*

NEAREST POINT OF RELIEF
This is an important issue relating to the correct procedure when taking a free drop. It describes the exact spot, no nearer the hole, where the obstruction or condition ceases to be a problem.

NET SCORE
This is arrived at by taking the gross score minus the golfer's handicap. So, if a 13-handicap golfer gets around the course in 82 strokes, the net score is 69.

OBSTRUCTIONS
This term applies to anything artificial, such as an empty soda can, cigarette butt, or even a golf cart. For the most part, golfers are entitled to relief from obstructions if they interfere with play – much as with loose impediments.

OUT OF BOUNDS
Where no golfer wants to tread. This is an area of the course where play is prohibited, marked by white lines or stakes.

OUTSIDE AGENCY

This is anything that is not part of the match or, in stroke play, not a part of the competitor's side. An obvious example would be, say, a greenkeeper's mower (*see also* Rub of the green).

PAY-AS-YOU-PLAY

Public golf courses where the casual visitor can turn up and play, without having to fulfill any membership requirements.

PITCH MARK

Indentation made on the green where the ball lands.

PITCH-MARK REPAIRER

Forklike tool designed for repairing the damage caused to the putting surface when a ball lands on it.

PLAY THROUGH

If any group fails to keep up with the general pace of play, loses ground on the group ahead, or loses a ball, then the group behind should immediately be invited to play through. Beware, this is not merely a common courtesy.

You can actually be penalized for repeated slow play.

PROVISIONAL BALL

If you hit a shot and suspect that your ball might be lost, you can, and indeed are, encouraged to play a provisional ball. This is basically a timesaving measure, as the provisional ball becomes the ball in play if your original ball cannot be found.

QUALIFYING COMPETITION

A competition in which a golfer's handicap can go up or down, depending on how they perform.

REASONABLE EVIDENCE

In order to declare a ball lost in a hazard, there must be "reasonable evidence." A splash of water is normally "reasonable evidence" but not always – see Decision 26-1/1.

THE ROYAL & ANCIENT GOLF CLUB OF ST. ANDREWS (R&A)

Formerly the Society of St. Andrew Golfers, this group in 1897 extended the original rules of golf to a more comprehensive code of rules. Now responsible for administering the Rules of Golf and making decisions on these rules for golfers all over the world, except in the United States, and Mexico, where the USGA has jurisdiction.

RUB OF THE GREEN

This occurs when a ball is deflected or stopped by an outside agency. No penalty is incurred and you play the ball as it lies, but unfortunately rub of the green works both ways. For instance, if your ball bounces off a greenkeeper's tractor straight into a pond beside the green, that's bad luck. Likewise, though, if your ball hits the same tractor and bounces into the hole, that's a good rub of the green and the shot stands – you won't be needing your putter.

SPIKE MARKS

Damage to the green caused by the spikes on golf shoes. It is against the Rules to repair such marks on the line of your putt, but as a consideration to other players it is always a good idea to tap down obvious spike marks around the hole after you've putted out.

STABLEFORD COMPETITION

A stroke-play event where points are awarded for each hole. One point for a bogey, two points for a par, three points for a birdie, four points for an eagle, and five points for that rarest of birds, an albatross.

STROKESAVERS

Common name for yardage books in Europe.

TEEING GROUND

The starting point for every hole, defined by tee markers on either side and encompassing an area two club-lengths deep.

THROUGH THE GREEN

Not quite as simple as it sounds. It can mean literally too long; but its definition is much more all-encompassing. It includes the whole area of the course, except the teeing ground and putting green of the hole being played, and any hazards on the course.

TOP DRESSING

A dressing of soil mixture applied and brushed into the surface of the green. Light and frequent top dressing helps create smooth puting surfaces.

UNITED STATES GOLF ASSOCIATION (USGA)

The governing body in the United States and Mexico responsible for administering the Rules of Golf.

UNPLAYABLE LIE

Any number of situations on the golf course, the important point being that you are the sole judge of whether a ball is unplayable. There are several relief options available, under penalty, once you have declared that your ball is unplayable.

WATER HAZARDS

A water hazard may or may not contain water but will be marked with either red or yellow stakes or lines. The relief procedures for the two have subtle differences (*see pages 86 to 89*). It pays to know your water.

WINTER RULES

A set of codes that come into force during the winter months. Generally speaking, they allow golfers preferred lies on the fairway and relief from a plugged ball in the rough.

WINTER RULES *will be in effect if the course is snowed under.*

Acknowledgments

There are many who have given me valuable assistance in the
compilation of this book, but I owe a particular vote of thanks to
David Lamb, Frank Ritter, and Derek Coombes of DK for their
encouragement during the project, and to Arthur Brown and
Alistair Plumb of Cooling Brown for their ideas and illustrative input.
I owe a special debt of gratitude to David Rickman, Rules Secretary of the
Royal & Ancient Golf Club, for his keeping me on the straight and narrow
in matters of the Rules. Finally, without the help and encouragement
of Jane McCandlish the project would not have been completed.

The Rules of Golf are © The Royal & Ancient Golf Club of St. Andrews.
Dorling Kindersley is grateful for permission to publish extracts.

Dorling Kindersley would like to thank the following for their
assistance in the creation of this book:
Doug McClelland and Eric Wheeley at The Doug McClelland Golf
Superstore, Silvermere, Surrey, UK and Terry Conebar, for the loan of
equipment; Mike Tapsell (Club Secretary) and Members of the North
Middlesex Golf Club for their patience during photography; Vic Newell,
Chantel Newell, and Mel Simmons for their modeling talents; and
Steve Newell and James Harrison for editorial input.

Picture Credits

Useful Addresses

Additional information on handicapping and publications
are available from:
United States: The United States Golf Association,
P.O. Box 708, Far Hills, New Jersey 07931-0708.
Britain & Europe: The National Council of Golf Unions,
Formby Golf Club, Formby, Liverpool, E37 1LQ, England.
The Ladies' Golf Union, The Scores, St. Andrews, Fife,
KY16 9AT, Scotland.